CLEAR CREEK

CLEAR CREEK
The Heart of the Rippling World

Essays on the Shapes of Nature

Judson D. McGehee

GLEN
LYON
PRESS

The essays in this book originally appeared in "Northland Nature" in the *Arizona Daily Sun*.

Glen Lyon Press, LLC
Flagstaff, Arizona
Visit our website at ***www.glenlyonpress.com***

CLEAR CREEK
Copyright © 2014 by Judson D. McGehee

For information address Glen Lyon Press, LLC.

Front Cover Photograph: Daniel Goman/Dreamstime.com

ISBN: 978-0-692-23327-6

In loving memory of Ottilie 'Lee' McGehee

To be admitted to Nature's hearth costs nothing. None is excluded, but excludes himself. You have only to push aside the curtain.

— Henry David Thoreau

CONTENTS

A FEW FOREWORDS

THESE ESSAYS are labors of love and the result of sensory awareness, mental clarity, and a cultivated absorption in what is to be seen and touched and wondered at. I read the cinders that lie in the depths of a desert wash and steep myself in prose that hurts—prose by writers like Eiseley and Leopold and Lopez, prose of conceptual complexity and of lyric simplicity, prose like a thunderstorm and the slow drip of rain. When I wish to grieve or exult, when I wish to become another thing and elsewhere, I turn to words of imaginative intensity, to words with pulse and purity.

These words strive to objectify nature, to let it speak for itself. Even if hurried, the phrase must sound. Words are pebbles, gull feathers, oak leaves. Their emotional and creative value depends upon the reader's past experience with them, with ferns and feathers and stones. I value economy and insight, euphony and detail, honest emotion. My style shifts with the wind, turns with the point of view like a weather vane.

Having wandered as a child, I am now, like

a mesquite, rooted in a small corner of the Colorado Plateau. My landscapes are varied—lonesome and angular, pastoral and painterly, down canyon and upland. There is always a hawk overhead, a tree on the horizon. I wish to convey what I feel when the land wells up like tears inside me. I find I have a sense of kinship with the land and its life forms. The land holds my heart because it takes the shape of law and shelters life. Fay Canyon, in the stillness of its half-light, sings with the small voice of a cricket, echoes with the evening call of a thrush.

The land in its vastness is never indifferent because intelligence lies at the heart of matter, and form itself is a form of spirit. Were matter dead, life could not have arisen from it. Rarely am I granted a sense of the numinous; the secrets I learn are trivial and for the taking. The shapes of nature, the forms of life, support a lifetime of study. Seeking and seeing is enough.

WEST CLEAR CREEK

1. Promise

I shall walk with water
I shall bend my head by Clover Spring
kneel in the long grass beside its creek
I shall arise and walk westward.

I shall stand in silence
at the Valley of the Willow
I shall laugh with my second name
and my steps shall be swift
swift as clear water.

I shall walk with beauty on my left hand
the changes of Meadow Canyon
I shall hold Buckhorn in my right
my feet shall flow between two mountains
the mountain of cedar
the mountain of black rock
and I shall sing
"the leaf of the earth is my leaf
and all that belongs to the earth belongs to me
the sycamore and his moonlit limbs
the ribbed edge of the plunging water
the water round stones
all things."

Clear Creek

I shall rest in the sun on Cactus Mountain
I shall stand at last on the edge of the mesa
while birds wing over the yellow field
my eyes will be green like the river's water
and my hands will be heavy with praise
as the winter wind my voice will be clear.

2.   Prayer

May all things begin in beauty
and through the returning seasons
may I walk.

May I walk in November
giving thanks
in old age wandering on a trail of water
living again and lively.

May I walk
walk with water
with grasshoppers about my feet
alive in the litter
of summer spent leaves.

ON MIDDLE EARTH

NOON. We flush robins from sycamore to sycamore. A long-tailed accipiter, lean, hawkish, and heavily barred, dips between thickets of mesquite. Though Clear Creek runs past the pale gold of winter grasses, the first week of spring is in everything—in the tiger swallowtail that circles us like Raggedy Ann's golden butterfly; in the budding alders whose twigs, still tipped with last year's cones, slowly unfold their strongly veined, infant-perfect leaves. Rooted in a wall of volcanic rock, the cove-sheltering, white-limbed sycamore stirs in a restless sleep. The pool below us is transparent in the steady sun, cobbled with old stones, deep and current-cold. As if we have entered Rivendell or Lórien, an easy enchantment seems to halo this crescent of sand.

Unhurried as the slow passage of the sun, my wife Lee and I tend to the small care of our campsite, place stones for our grill on the damp earth edging the waters. A few yards upstream, a root mass has trapped a dam of twigs and squaw wood—sun-dried flotsam to tender our supper fire.

After a taste of Tang and pressed ham, honey and home-baked bread, we lie in leisure. The sun finds us susceptible, and, like unwintering bears, we slowly unlayer. The sand is summer hot and sifts easily between our toes. Time has abandoned us. We are left with life.

Out of the juniper-thrashing, weed-tumbling wind, and breathing the constant harmony of the rapids, we lower ourselves into the water. Trout-like we cleave the current. Stung by the cold, I grasp a knotted, tree-tied rope, raise myself into the warm, alien, unlifting air, then fall back heavily into the more natural depths, limpid, lovely, and less chill.

Warm again on the sand, we watch the daystar dip toward Wingfield Mesa, its light still falling on the stream bank where it shelves down to the leaf-littered shore. My mind swims out to the heart of this rippling world of clean green trout, this pool that the creek has carved in its finger-crooked curve to escape the spur of Cactus Mountain.

TWILIGHT. Inchling trout rise to bubble the surface like evening rain. Their dimples fan out in flurries then die away like the hoot of the great horned owl that now calls from across the canyon. He persists in his natural announcement—a deep, downsoft, "Hoo, hoo-hooo . . . hoo, hoo-hooo."

Lee and I share chicken casserole, hot chocolate, and sesame bars. As our fire flickers low, I feed it a few smooth limbs. We lie back upon the down of our sleeping bag, awake to the young stars and to the high and horizontal crescent of the moon that sways in the dark sea like a silver ship.

NIGHT. In the abandonment of night, the branched rope sways in the canyon's wind. Upper, middle, and lower worlds all come alive in the spun-warm and spindled dark and weave our linked thoughts. The sun-closed cosmic window lies open at last. We gaze up and down, into a water world of stars. I see Orion in his belted magnificence, with his Big Dog at heel. Their great fires burn so far away we feel nothing of their fury, and our own little fire embers out at our feet. We cannot grasp the space, the immense waste of that distant world, but it has awakened something in us.

And other creatures from the lower world are rising restless; out of the starred waters of the pool, young trout begin to leap. One slaps the surface like a flat-tossed stone. Another rockets up into the alien element, hangs for an instant of harsh joy, then falls back. And we, who also live at the bottom of a sea, launch thought after thought up to the surface of Middle Earth, only to have them return like astronauts in a splashdown of momentary wonder.

COYOTE SONG

THE SKY WAS LAVENDER. Long shadows of evening dulled the boles of the clustered aspen that stood in silent, full-leafed glades along lower Weatherford Canyon. My family walked along the forest road a hundred yards to my left, and I was just about to head back in their direction. Suddenly I stood rooted in surprise. My skin prickled as if I were touching a live wire.

Without forewarning and quite close at hand, the loud, clear yip-yap of a coyote merged into a shrill cry that seemed intense enough to stir the pines on the slopes of Schultz Peak. I could feel the tremolo, the quaver in the animal's voice, but I could not tell if his evening call was of anger or of ecstasy. I suspect that, aware of my presence, he sang simply to assert his own wild identity.

Fire leaps up the twiggy tinder and feeds on the broken branches I give it, while a talc and gunmetal moon rises behind pines that ride the eastern ridge. The goddess glows with a reflected light that blots out all but the brightest stars.

As we savor chunks of stewed beef and fork up the last of the oriental noodles, from down road comes a startling sound—a repeated hoop or whup that is too loud for an owl. Though vaguely hound-like, it does not suggest the bark of a domestic dog.

As I stand listening to each rasping bark, I am excited by a sense of mystery that is not unmixed with fear. At last I conclude that these sounds are the muted yaps and yips of a coyote. The full moon and its slow rising have not passed unnoticed.

Lee and I listen in awed silence to a hymn to the recurring mystery of the moon, the great-eyed sky mother of all wild things. Staccato yelps, varying in tone, soon give rise to more rapid and higher pitched barks. Statements intensely urged, they suggest the god-awakening cries of the Yei Be Chei Singers as the dancers shuffle and chant through the long last night of the Navajo healing ceremony.

As the coyotes' excitement increases, their cries are briefly prolonged into howls that last at most two or three seconds. They are sharply pointed exclamations and not at all like the prolonged and spine-tingling howl of the timber wolf. But as suddenly as the barking began, it ends.

When supper is done and hot chocolate steams in our canteen cups, the chorus of the coyotes begins again. This time their cries are close enough to touch. The individual voice of each animal is clear. Like the light from a distant star, the sounds are resolved into their component parts—an audible spectrum. I search out the six-volt lantern lest their curiosity overcome their normal fear of man and lead them down the slope to our faltering campfire.

Though it is well known that a coyote's rapid falsetto can sound as if several animals sing in chorus, two distinct individuals seem to produce this last cascade of notes. One bark is lower in pitch, with a darker timbre. The other is shriller and more exclamatory. The emotional quality of the combination is difficult to describe. The sounds are strident but not angry, serious but not sad, earnest but uncomplaining. Their night song is spirited and natural, the essence of the wild.

I picture them as dog and vixen. Mated for life, together they call to the mottled disk of the indifferent moon. Their own voices re-echo from ridge and canyon—as if the sky god answers them.

LOCH NESTA

OUR EASTWARD PROGRESS blocked by a ravine, Lee and I descend to the sandstone inner canyon. We help each other down the abrupt drop of a dry falls and enter a streamside sanctuary of rolled stones and white sand. Taking Lee's pack, I lean it against a ledge of rust-red rock that juts out from the cliff behind us. I kneel to drop my own beside it.

Unburdened, tired but excited, we are lured eastward by the call of the rapids. The bank along the south shore narrows to nothing. There can be no further progress without fording the creek. Returning downstream, we pick our way along a fisherman's path a few feet above slow moving shallows that are gray from a slit of fine sand and leaf mold.

Above my head a warbler, yellow-breasted and olive-backed, flits about the branches of a willow. A mourning dove sighs in the distance. Tough-stemmed shrubbery drives us inland till we find a second trail around grape-hung alders and below white-limbed sycamores. Angular slabs of sandstone that have been plucked from the cliff face lie lodged in deep sand. We detour around them only to encounter a tangle of fallen timbers. As we pick our way across them, unseen behind its veil of greenery, the creek pulses in our ears.

Life loves light and water, I think to myself. Here in this creek bed, a host of living things have gathered—a whole creation just for us. I have a feeling that something important lies ahead—something as numinous as stone, as eloquent as water. Surmounting a ledge above bare roots and wedged rocks, we pause, breathless from exertion and discovery.

A dark green pool, half in shade, half in sunlight, lies in a long trench of stone. Walled on the south by an unclimbable cliff, it seems deep enough to hide the Loch Ness Monster. Lee and I are awed by its beauty and seclusion. Reflected on its surface is a leaf-green arcade of over-reaching branches. From a deciduous woodland along the north shore, alders, willows, and cottonwoods have joined with velvet ash and water birch to create a living wall of foliage. Their roots, snake-like, thrust out from the low and cobbled bank. A shaft of overhead sun lightens a poolside ledge.

No human architect could have created a setting so perfect or a pool so inviting. Come, enter, it seems to say. Be one with light and shadow, sun and stone, leaf and water. We are discoverers of an older, darker, and richer world, and we recognize in the tiny, face-hovering flies, winged representatives of the sacred serpent that dwells in the heart of every Eden.

The pool—Loch Nesta we are quick to name it—lies between the yang of the sandstone cliff and the yin of the leaf-dark shore. A few small trout rise to swirl a surface that supports a shoal of silver-winged gnats. Stone-impeded, the white sound of water surrounds us with a double sense of protection. Through breaks in the leaf-hung canopy, a track of blue shows us we are open to the world of hawks and herons, tells us that the sun comes here as a stranger and is soon to leave.

Having surveyed the borders of our world, we walk back to make our campsite in the sand. When still deep in the cliff-shaded defile, we hear a high-pitched whistle. Both plaintive and shrill, the call seems to be that of a hawk hidden by the treetops. Suddenly a thick-winged Buteo circles above our heads. His yellow bill opens with each nasal cry. Solidly black from below, he has a rounded tail that is both tipped and banded with white. This pool's guardian spirit, then, is a Mexican black hawk.

Setting up camp is a simple task for two backpackers with only a sleeping bag and a rainfly. It takes but a moment to find a slab of sandstone upon which to set our stove. As I begin to lift a piece that is part of an abandoned fireplace, it shifts slightly to the left and a slate-gray lizard leaps from beneath it, then darts down into the safety of a crevice. I feel a stab of anguish as I see its mate, squeezed by the pivoting stone, lying upon its back, belly torn and mouth distended in a silent scream.

I place the stone to one side and watch as the dying lizard, in a last instinctive effort, tightens the muscles at the base of its tail. It pops off like a champagne cork to assume a separate but short-lived existence. A slender and active worm, it whips and writhes with a motion designed to attract the eye of a predator. The lizard swallows one last time, blood staining the corners of its mouth, then stiffens. But the tail continues its distracting dance for minutes afterward.

Its mate crouches quietly in the shade of rock, a foot below the scene of the disaster. Saddened by my fatal intrusion into their innocent lives, I pause to ponder the imponderables, unable to guess at the extent of a reptile's understanding. Knowing that my action was inadvertent, I can identify it with rockslides, flashfloods, or the sudden, sharp-hoofed trampling of a mule deer.

It was fate that brought me here—I speak

this in my mind over the dead lizard—one of the inevitable accidents of life that caught and crushed you.

Because I want the survivor to know what happened, I take the stained and stiffened body and place it beside its motionless mate. This is the second time, to my knowledge, that I have killed a lizard by lifting a stone. My former feelings, remembered, mix with these fresh ones; but I am consoled by the fact that whiptails are as common as black flies along the banks of this creek, and that life will go on like a rippling flow of water into which a single leaf has fallen and whirled away.

RAIN WALK

THE HALF LIGHT of gathering cumulus conspires with the summer-rich leafage to shadow the canyon trail. Far above our heads, a thunder cell is breeding, sucking in its breath till it can hold no more. I'm glad that Lee carries, beside the tent strapped to the top of her Jansport, two wet-weather ponchos.

It seems long till we reach the first carved and varnished post—one-half mile. Amid the confusion of trails, a fitful rain begins to fall, most of it caught by the needles and leaves that block our view of the canyon rim. The dying light and distant rumble of storm darken the pale freshness of fern, dull the spikes of blue lupine and the luster of yellow monkey flowers. Even the warm reds and oranges of scarlet penstemon and paintbrush seem chilled.

Like the insects, we are reluctant to take cover, savoring each ray of fugitive sun. A five-petaled flower, white streaked with violet, is a favorite stopping place for honeybees. Solitary and bear-like, a bumblebee breaks in among them. Delicate flyers, small butterflies with coppery brown on their forewings, bright orange on their hind, lighten the air with their presence. A trio of mourning cloaks, unexpectedly large by comparison, drift in the sea-green light. Bold in their tree-tip flutterings, western tiger swallowtails sway and tack like sloops in a crosswind. Their giant size makes even the mourning cloaks seem small. New to my eye are a race of middle-sized, soot-gray butterflies. Social and thirsty, they gather in black covens at the edge of streambank seepage and along the damp sandstone of the ledge-lined creek.

Whenever the sky darkens with cloud, a robin carols—the canyon's twilight singer. Our voices hushed by the underbrush of dogwood and shrub oak, ferns and horsetails, we circle fellings of Douglas fir or stop to admire a giant pine that the path respectfully circles.

Though we have started late and wish to be five miles up West Fork by nightfall, we are relaxed, unhurried, accepting. When the rain finally thickens and strikes us a full blow, we don our ponchos and hike on, drenched below the knees by glistening fronds of broadleaf plants. Lee bends a branch in passing, and wet leaves slap my face. As I follow less closely, I wonder where the frail wings rest when the leaf-rattling rain descends. Our feet are as soaked as if we had waded through the creek. If we miss the stepping stones at the ford, it makes no difference now.

I stand in the steady drizzle and watch the darting of a trout along a knife-edged trough of sandstone. His pool is only a wetter world than ours. With amazing speed, he vanishes below an overhang of shrub willow and comes to rest under a rock in the lee of a hummock of stout grass.

Now rapids roar above the pelt and sting of rain, wet joining wet. How seasonal the canyon is, how utterly altered by its plant life! Though I recognize the purple stems of red osier dogwood, now fully leafed, and the legions of light-hungry Gambel oak that lean into the trail and contest our passage, this seems like my first hike up West Fork. The trail masked by foliage, we miss the caves where we usually lunch. I imagine a conspiracy of elf-like people, Celtic Trailbenders, whose pleasure it is to shift each landmark as we pass by.

For a time I wonder whether, in the rain-early dark, Lee and I have not blundered onto some side-canyon trail. But our home, plus a change of clothes and shoes, is on our backs; and, warm with this knowledge, we plow right on as dark consumes the canyon.

The storm reaches its height in sharp volleys of thunder. With the roar of a hundred-car freight, wind rushes up the canyon, blurring the trees about us. Yet the patter and ping of rain and the gleam of washed rocks bring a feeling of innocence. We feel safe and close, deep in the heart of the heart of this canyon, while six hundred feet above us stands a balanced rock carved like the head of a tribal elder.

The chords of high and flashless thunder grow more distant and spaced. The rain tapers to a mist as we reach a dry and sandy, cliff-carved cave. It has been a rich and highland walk, and we savor the sweetness of camp, the end of effort.

The birds sing morning into being. I remember, in my half sleep, dozing off to the solemn "rrrrr's" of a tree frog who may still cling with rubber toes to a rain-wet curve of sandstone. In my mind, minnows slip through sunlit shoals of pebbled creek, but when I open my eyes and loosen the ties to the ventilating window, I can see, through the white nylon mesh, that the sky is still curdled and sea gray.

I remember yesterday's rain walk up West Fork—the chill of wet trouser legs and sopping socks; and I savor the delicious warmth of well-fluffed down, sun-dry nylon, and the breath-lovely ambience of Lee beside me and asleep.

How far did the Hiking Club go that year, I wonder. I see again the beaver dam, hold in both hands the yellow-incisored skull, relive the iconed peace of those great orange walls. And here I am again, years later, and the beauty, though different, is just as intense.

I slip from the tent, watch leaves drip in the cool silence, feel the moist air against my legs, the dawn light pure as spring water. I stand in a daze of pleasure, contemplate the steady art that decked with slabs of sandstone the mounded flanks of the fire pit. I glance at the flotsam-wedged timber, slanting against the half dome of red rock, where five pair of athletic socks are lined up and stretched out to dry. At this hour no sun delves into the canyon here, and our wet and sandy jeans still hang like spoiled fruit from an overburdened alder.

Movement feels good to sleep-stiffened limbs as I follow footprints through the sand along the inner edge of the cliff whose overhang has created this sanctuary. The path leads, with some slippery footing, to the forested bench above us.

Back again beside our tent, I stand barefoot in the shade-cool sand, careful to preserve Lee's well-earned sleep. Flowers and foliage seem thankful for yesterday's drought-ending rain, and, as I walk down the path to the creek, I brush through thickets that baptize me with brief showers from broad, rain-jeweled leaves. Innocent of the stiff spines and sharp barbs of desert shrubs, the pliant stems of these streambank bushes and young trees yield to my passage till I stand in the rippling waters of the creek.

Sun has begun its descent into the canyon, and I am fully awake, alive to all water spun, leaf mould, and stony delights. Filled with an inner stillness, I return with the soup pot and prepare to light the Sportsman stove.

THE SACRED DATURA

I RISE AT DAWN from our dew-stained tent.
The air is cool and thick with the trembling of
the storm-swollen stream. Cliff-shadow moss
lies fat in the creases of an old rockfall that is
half covered by a sprawl of canyon grape. The
draw between Cedar Mountain and Lizard
Peak is deep in shadow, but the rim of the
canyon rings with a light that halos the spent
stalks of agave and the rank and mule-eared
colonies of prickly pear.

As I walk east in search of firewood, a white
rag on a bush catches my eye. Curious, I
investigate, but am unprepared for this sight.
A waist-high, sprawling, gray-green shrub that
is half bush, half vine has produced a single
perfect bloom—a hauntingly beautiful and
unnaturally large trumpet-shaped flower.
White with pale purple edges, it is horned and
triple-veined along each of its five sides.

As I bend to examine it, I find its fragrance
lethargic and vaguely evil. I count the five

yellow-tipped stamens that encircle the pistil, then sketch the leaves on a page of my field journal. They are ovate, strongly-scented and velvet to the touch because of an undercoat of fine hairs. Each leaf is on a petiole, and the stems and twigs are purplish, the lower stalks woody.

Finally, using the ruled edge of my note pad, I measure the blossom. Including the green sheath at the base of the corolla, the flower is a tropical nine inches long and four inches in diameter. Inspection of the plant reveals several collapsed and wilting blooms and the beginnings of a round, prickle-covered seedpod.

Before I call Lee to share my discovery, I pause, overtaken by a sense of ancient and mysterious beauty, forbidden powers. I know this plant, a member of the nightshade family, is as poisonous as it is impressive, and a voice inside my head chants three sacred syllables—"Datura, Datura, Datura." I feel like the primitive who first tamed fire—undecided whether what I had taken into my home was friend or foe, angel or devil.

In the still air of this early-morning canyon, I sense the presence of an ancient god: a hallucinogenic plant that men of many races and times have worshipped and used—grinding the tiny brown seeds to add to fermented drinks, steeping the leave and twigs in water, or powdering the dried roots.

Datura, you have been with us through centuries of ritual divinations and inspired prophecies, coming of age ceremonials and sacred frenzies. The Delphic Oracle has spoken through your intoxicating smoke. Through you we have petitioned for rain and fertility, for healing powers and divine knowledge. You and your sister species have stupefied the wives and slaves of battle-slain warriors before they were led to their master's grave. The rain priests of the Zunis have seen with your eyes and, rooted to the soul of the sky, have talked with the old dead, asking for intercession. Yuman and Yokuts, Aztec and Tarahumara, aboriginal and modern, have tasted your toxins and learned from your madness.

Now, back at my study desk with books spread in a half circle beside me, I am confronted, like Faust, by the inadequate facts. I read that the plant's most active hallucinogens are the tropane alkaloids hyoscyamine and scopolamine. I read also that not too long ago a man in California died from drinking the juice, and that children have perished from eating the seeds or sickened from sucking the nectar from the flowers.

I learn that Datura, like a troll or a Halloween ghost, has blossoms that do not love the light, opening only in the early evening and closing at the touch of the sun.

But one truth remains, Datura—you are beautiful, baleful, dear and deadly, potent and poisonous, and in your restless and vision-filled sleep, the hollow-voiced gods have appeared, and they have spoken of things to come.

THE MOUNTAINS
OF THE MIND

WHEN ONE HAS SEEN enough and that which has been seen has lain in the mind, been worked by the alchemy of the brain into images, and then, in the moment when sleep first thins, the images return transformed into landscapes that never were, but for the dreamer are more real and more deeply experienced than any ever seen—when this happens, one has climbed the mountains of the mind.

In my sleep I see a redstone canyon, raw and eroded, devoid of vegetation, and as close to a dream as the heart comes, as close to the heart as a dream comes. A stark land whose layered and crumbling form lies buried in the heart of the stone. Every rain reveals more of it, and it is always the same. Every wind rubs the surface away to show the surface beneath. A primal and Platonic pattern, it lies in the dreaming mind changeable and beyond change, and is a joy that colors my waking and blesses the whole of my day.

In my dream I follow a dry wash deep into the lunar hills till walls of ribbed and buttressed sandstone rise on either hand. Side canyons have left rapids of broken rock that I slowly circle. The ridge to my right is leanly spired with basalt.

The trail as I remember it—and the imagery of a dream, no matter how precise when experienced, is blurred in memory—conveys a sense of transcendent reality. I pass an occasional sill of intrusive rock, a veined and marbled granite, but the cliffs, in their pale reds and oranges, suggest Coconino sandstone.

I enter a narrow passage, the walls of dreamstone cool to the touch. Perhaps, I am in Redbud Pass on the landward way to Rainbow Bridge. Here, there is water trapped in waist-deep pools linked by short cascades. I must swim to travel farther. The water is clear and chill and has the same lifeless beauty as the stone it has shaped.

Dripping with cold, I arise from the last of the pools to walk along a bench of burnished rock. Red, tan, gray, and white, stream-worn cobbles lie scattered on its shining surface. The creek makes a small sound as it falls from hollow to hollow, swirls in shallow potholes.

Ahead is the abrupt end of a box canyon. At the foot of the cliff, the creek tunnels out between faulted strata. Without thought or hesitation, I plunge into the quick water and swim into the heart of the mountain.

Now the image fades and memory invokes an older and repeated dream. A foot trail circles through an alpine landscape lying at the base of a granite ridge. The long stone mountain is as high as Half Dome and intricately weathered and ravined. The rock seems to be a pale Sierra granite, but the domes and the spires suggest Pinnacles National Monument. While the mountainous ridge rises above tree line, the lower slopes are mottled by a Krummholz of prostrate shrubs and trees.

My path winds between split stones and white-bark pines as it ascends in switchbacks to a level bench broken by talus from the cliffs above. As I travel eastward, on my left lies the steep rise of the mothering mountain; on my right, sun-silvered playas far in the hazy distance of a tableland that is salt pale and cloud purple.

The trail divides, and I realize that there is a way, to the left and up the slope, that I've never taken before. The path ahead keeps to the mountain's shoulder and reaches, in three miles, a hanging valley, half meadow, half woods, where an abandoned stone house, like a small Scottish castle, stands in ruins. Behind weathered, fieldstone walls lies an algae-rank pond that harbors the dimly aquatic shapes of creatures unknown to man's science.

In previous dreams I've always stayed on this lower trail. The summit, I know, is wild—a place where one can find bighorn sheep, a mountain lion, the winter den of a marmot, the nest of a golden eagle. Today I choose the left hand trail and wilderness views that will burn my heart away. Where I begin to climb, the path is mossed and shadowed by monoliths of granite.

It is a wind-bright April day, and melt-water flows down runnels of rock, flares over faces of slanting stone, and awakens the roots of moss campion and avalanche lily. Somewhere amid the wilderness peaks above me, a woman stands at the terraced mouth of a cave that winds deep into the heart of the mountain and holds secrets that have never seen the light of day. Her limbs are as smooth as water-loved stone and her long hair shines in the sun.

CLIFF DREAMS

CLIFF-DWELLER dreams—every time one returns I think that someday, perhaps, it will be more than a dream, that someday I will fashion that foolish actuality. But if not or never, the dream itself is enough.

In this dream, a man and a woman live together in a sunlit dwelling with slab-stone and clay-chinked walls and juniper-smoked ceilings—an authentic Sinagua site not unlike Walnut Canyon or Tuzigoot.

A footpath leads up ledges to their high rock home. Here the young couple lives with idyllic indifference to time and a pure commitment to the moment as it unfolds. Peace floods their senses like the blue ambience of high-desert air, or like river water that sparkles in a hand-hoed ditch and darkens the root soil of maize and beans.

Before the walled inner cave is an airy ledge, a south-facing platform, smooth as river-worn stone. Since their cliff dwelling is ideally situated, they strive to keep its existence a secret from hunters who may wander through their canyon.

They cook over a fire of split juniper, pinyon, and thicket oak. They sleep on the deeply furred pelts of gray fox, black bear, and mountain sheep. On chill nights they lie under robes of loosely corded rabbit fur. A persistent spring glides darkly down their cliff from the wooded mesa above.

The woman wears a fringed kilt of gray-white buckskin and a double necklace of disk shells strung with turquoise and coral. On her feet are ankle-high moccasins with rawhide soles and buckskin uppers. He wears a cape of corded turkey feathers over his brown shoulders and a loincloth of native cotton. His feet are bare and strong.

Their long day is spent in unnatural leisure—a dream leisure that ignores the reality of a hunting and food-gathering people. Their large coiled baskets and finely spiraled, corrugated pots store sunflower seeds, pinyon and jojoba nuts, squawberries and hackberries, elderberries and chokecherries. A squirrel-skin pouch holds cactus-seed meal for pinole.

The dream shows the results of labor, but not the labor itself. No digging in hard ground for sego lily bulbs; no grinding of mano against metate. Nor is there the patient setting of snares and nets for birds and other small game. There are no mosquitoes, flies, or biting gnats on their unscreened terrace; and no problems with the disposal of human wastes.

They live beside squat and friendly jars of winnowed grass seeds and mesquite pods; they sit on plaited mats beneath strings of beaver and venison jerky. Over their thin fire murmurs a delicate stew of diced prairie dog, rabbit, and field mouse. It is savored with wild onions and thickened with blanched corn meal.

In one dream scene, there is a foot of snow on the ground, deep and white and wet. The air is misty with the cold of morning. Wearing a rabbit fur cloak and moccasins with leggings, the young man descends the path. He breaks a trail that follows the base of their cliff and continues up and over a ridge. Back tracking carefully, he sweeps the loose snow over his steps with the wind-broken bough of a pine.

In the dream, the young woman is never bored, is incapable of boredom. Yet each day she tests her courage by walking along a narrow ledge till it fades into the face of the cliff. She tells her companion that this risk renews her sense of life.

Their days are of shared and simple joys, of contemplating and observation. Thinking, he says, is better than acting, and feeling is better than thinking, and better than feeling is watching.

Together they watch the days turn and the

Clear Creek

nights fall and the far stars shine. Friendship and love leaven the tasks of food preparation and fuel gathering.

On bright days they swim, hunt, or wander their homeland; or they practice the minor domestic arts—finger weaving, shell stringing, pottery making.

It is a pretty dream—harmless, unreal, impractical. But it is the nature of a dream to be a vision of the ideal, not a confrontation with the real. It is the way a mind imagines life might be.

Through the dream's varied and repeated scenes runs the theme of shared solitude in a wilderness setting. The feeling is one of ineffable and piercing sweetness, a sense of wholeness, harmony, and light.

Life is good, the cliff dream says.

50

DAWN WALK TO THE RIVER

A NIGHT BROKEN by sudden bursts of wind. The dawn is cold. With the frontal passage, the wind has slackened and shifted to the north. To the east, the sky is curdy with low and layered clouds that reflect the colors of the hidden sun, muted shades of lavender, pink, and rose.

Lee and I enter a shallow wash that begins on the slope below our tent. Here we meet a young desert cottontail as he feeds on the fresh stems and new leaves of shadscale. His coat is a mottled grayish brown, his ears are long, and his tail short but conspicuous, the white underside starkly visible in the half-light.

He stops nibbling and watches us till we are only ten feet away, then turns and hops slowly to our left, pausing every few feet to see if we intend to follow. Wary but not yet frightened, he behaves as if Lee and I are some strange new form of animal—as indeed we are. When we turn in his direction, he becomes alarmed and bounds up the terraced slope and over the sandstone ridge.

His instinct is to dash to any thicket or burrow he can find, and if he manages to live more than two years in the wild, it will be because his prey-sharp senses have warned him of those predators—coyotes, gray foxes, bobcats, owls, snakes, hawks, and golden eagles—that count on his species for food.

As the wash deepens, the way becomes rougher, and I miss the full horizon views. We climb a slope to our right, stepping over seedling plants that press up between broken fragments of stone, and pause on the crest. Though the sky is brighter, the sun is still hidden. A primitive road, marked by the fresh treads of a pickup truck, descends the draw to the south and seems bent, as we are, on reaching the river. We follow it.

Though other jeep trails join or leave ours, the archetypal attraction of water leads us unerringly eastward. The wash deepens to a narrow ravine, but the road, skirting a dry falls at the head of the gorge, ascends the south slope, parallels the creek bed, then descends where the wash fans out onto the floodplain of the Little Colorado.

Gray ranch buildings lie on the far slope a hundred yards to the north—an unpainted house, weathered stables, and a large corral fenced with juniper posts and four strands of barbed wire. The corral and stables are empty, the house deserted. A light wind lifts the alkaline dust.

Past the ranch, the road divides, one branch curving to the northwest, the other to the southeast, towards a water tank and the river. When the right-hand track shies away from a mile-long fence, we abandon it to scale a sand and stream-stone mound. From this height we can trace the sinuous northward course of the river. Sun-cracked and lime-crusted marshes bordered by thickets of tamarisk, desert willow, and occasional cottonwoods.

The wire strands of the fence are strong enough to be climbed, and, once safely over, we pick up the first cow path that leads east. Rank marsh grasses vie with twiggy, dead-black mesquite and thorny shrubs to bar our passage. The alluvial clay is strewn with organic flotsam, coated with the lime-white scum of rotted plants and flood-borne froth.

We follow the deeply-plunged hoof prints of a single steer on its way to water. The riparian soil has been quick to dry following the river's retreat, and our path cannily circles the denser thickets and dips under the finely-leaved and drooping stems of the tamarisks.

Finally, firm sand brings us to the river. The Little Colorado is not so little this morning, but two hundred yards wide and seemingly shallow enough to wade. The rusty-yellow current swirls swiftly, churns about clumps of sand willow, and races over shoals. Long riffles show where the bottom is close and stony, and steep waves storm the shallows as eddies instress the murky surface. The river in its raw insistence, its dominance over its banks, represents an ancient force, seems alien and a little threatening. I am not the least tempted to cross.

Its broad, fast-flowing surface frames and intensifies the eastern landscape, lends the mystery of distance to the far shore. To the north, it begins its three-mile curve around the point of Baah Lokaa Ridge, where rounded buttes and mud-shale cliffs haze into the distance.

Lee and I sit together in the moist shade of a young cottonwood and share a granola bar breakfast while, circling about us, mosquitoes sing their rising song and an unseen Hereford lows moodily from the marsh.

As the day breaks golden at last, and our world is flooded with light, I remember the words of Mary, a fellow hiker. Yesterday she told us how her son had seemed to know that he was soon to die in a climbing accident, the mindless rock giving way beneath his hands. And when she finished, she turned to Lee and said, "The Irish cry when their children are born." As I watch the river now, I feel both her pain and her joy.

RETURN TO LOCH NESTA

WE PARK and don our packs in moonless midnight, uncertain about the water hazard ahead. The leap over the rush of the creek seems formidable until I attempt it. Then it becomes just another jump from wet, slanting rock, to damp, water-curved stone. Beyond the mid-stream boulder, last spring's stepping stones lie largely submerged. Our crossing is wet but safe.

We crawl under a creekside tangle of low branches, then cross wedged timber and water-round stones till we reach the far bank and a shrubby highland of grass and mesquite, pinyon and juniper.

The trail is plainly revealed by our flashlights, and we stride along single file through a warm and windless night. Fatigued but hopeful, we head inland rather than descend to the first ford. Though game trails meander along the terrace, no footpath appears to reassure us. The clumped grasses are tall and heavily arched. Shoulder-high branches of acacia claw at our windbreakers. We dodge to avoid the spines of yucca and agave.

I realize that I would never willingly hike in the dark through unfamiliar landscape. But I know this route well—the ground is level and the shadow of Lizard Peak steers us through the richly starred night.

At last we reach the high cliff that overlooks Loch Nesta. Defined by rapids to east and west, the pool itself is invisible, a dark and deeply centered stillness that swallows both light and thought. Can we descend to the creek? A ravine blocks our way, and, though we cautiously scout its banks, we can see no safe way down.

Finding a circle of soil clear of grass and free of stones—Lee suspects that it's an anthill—we unroll our ground cloth, pads, and sleeping bag. My high-powered binoculars rest beside me in their protective case, dreaming perhaps of stars. It will not be long before dawn, with its crescendo of bird calls, wakes us.

Bright carolings; clear whistles; cascades of notes descending; flute-like warblings; phoebe-faint lisps of sound. The canyon seems to have caught and concentrated all the avian life of a May morning between its high and lava-capped hills. Warblers congregate for the myriad insects that live in or near the water; unseen songbirds compete for nesting sites in the rich growth of riparian trees and shrubs.

Desert light floods the ravine and shows us the steeply slanting trail, with its unstable rocks and loose earth, that was hidden from us by night. We roll up our sleeping bag and thank the red ants who cleared the area of grass and whose tailings of fine sand filled and softened the surface. We shake a few early risers from the ground cloth as we fold it.

As we descend the ravine to the dry falls, it becomes clear that floodwaters have reshaped the beach along the creek's south bank. The sandy strip where we'd pitched our tent is now rocky and rutted. We leave our backpacks in the shade of a young velvet ash and set about applying insect repellant to forearms and hands, necks and faces. Loch Nesta's gnats are here to welcome us, just as they were last spring.

The Sportsman stove works well in this still, dense atmosphere, and water is soon ready for breakfast. When we finish, the sun leans over Lizard Peak and probably warms the sandstone ledges above the Loch. I unpack the beach bag, and we are off to greet the primal waters.

Loch Nesta proves to be the same unchanging paradise. Over-arching boughs of walnut and willow, alder and ash, canopy the creek. Mixed with them are taller sycamores and cottonwoods. Beneath the layers of deep sky and dense foliage lies the basal world of gray stones and red-rock cliffs where creek water glints and dazzles in the patchy, ever-shifting sun.

It is midweek, and this green haven of stone and air, light and water is purely ours. We take its gift of solitude and savor it with the thoughtful appreciation of connoisseurs. It promises idle hours and the exhilaration of deep, swift waters; it pledges moments of peace in sun-mottled shallows where fingerling trout drift and dart and flycatchers glean the living air.

As we rest in the late morning sun and rub our limbs with fragrant oil, I notice woody debris wedged in the branches of an Arizona walnut and a witches' broom of twigs caught in a cliff crevice ten feet above my head. The pool is nearly free of biting gnats—perhaps their rafts of eggs were washed away by the great high tide of spring.

Through my binoculars I watch the glinting curve of downhill water as its stressed surface swirls over the first great rocks of the rapids, then breaks into a celebration of leaping waves, air-whitened droplets, iridescent spray, and revolving galaxies of foam. The voice of the creek blesses the canyon, as newly leafed boughs dangle down like fire-fangled fronds of the palm at the end of my mind.

We breathe a mild and tawny daylight air till, oiled and steamy with the hour, we long to cool ourselves in the limpid waters. The Loch is spring cold and as swift and deep as love and death. My legs slide into the current till feet feel a slime-slick shelf of sandstone honed by the touch of water on its way through time. When my respiration slows, I sit in the full flow. Baptized by this buoyant world, I breast the length of light-dark Nesta. Lee sits in the shallows of the ledge, then commits herself to the chill waters of its nine-foot depths, to the shaping curves of its current. Together we swim and race, float and drift, dive and tumble like otters. When we grow tired and cold, we lie on the rust orange ledges above the pool and take the sun till the courage to return returns.

We break for lunch by our packs, then rest on our ground cloth in deep sand that high water has banked against the base of the cliff. Lizards watch us while the sun, leaf-green and dappled, dances beyond our eyes.

We pitch a tent that is too hot to enter, then, when the sun is low, set water on to boil. I tour the site, bird watching with my high-powered binoculars, and discover a young and flourishing sacred datura. I am happy to know that this evil and beautiful plant, divine, mystic, and deadly, continues to bless our Eden with its magnificent white blooms. Like Loch Nesta herself, the flower is light and dark, swift and still, and the flood of time will not uproot it.

STRAWBERRY CRATER

.

CINDERS SIFT UNDERFOOT and our progress is slow.

We rest on the narrow saddle, our packs under the thin branches of a juniper. To our right, a short steep rise to a pinnacle; to our left, a broken slope that leads up to a crescent ridge of roughly layered lava.

If there are ruins above us, there must be a way to reach them. We follow a faint trail around volcanic boulders and up over rubbled ledges. Nothing suggests the hand of man till we discover a low wall extending across a narrow ledge. Its upper tier is stained with the yellow-green of lichens that have grown there since the rocks were placed.

North of this wall is a broader ledge, level enough for a campsite. Beyond it is the first major ruin—a rectangular walled enclosure with an opening in the southwest corner. Though evenly floored with cinders, three of the four corners are marked by curious depressions. To the east and on a lower ledge, stands a cliff-backed shelter, half cave, half hand-built wall. Perched on the inner lip of Strawberry Crater, it suggests a sentry post. At neither site are there potsherds or other signs of habitation.

Fifty feet ahead of us, across a terraced ledge and built against a lava cliff, is a high-walled structure of closely fitted rocks. A three-quarter circle, it resembles an unroofed, ground-level kiva. Three carved steps lead up to the narrow, east-facing doorway. Within its head-high, curved, and wind-denying walls is a floor of cinders. Natural ledges and hollows on the cliff have left places for storage. A waist-high alcove in the northwest corner is a ready-made hearth for a ceremonial fire—a small but sacred flame.

Having found what we needed to find, a space to spread our sleeping bags, we return to the saddle for our packs. I bring back the twisted, bone-white branch of a pinyon pine—old wood for an after-supper fire.

While meteors flash through the Milky Way and the Andromeda Galaxy glows faintly beside Cassiopeia, I lay on the raised floor of the alcove a nest of bird-bone sticks, twigs, and splinters. As I touch a match to the tinder, it seems appropriate to speak a simple prayer. "Great Spirit, bless this fire and give peace to those who come in peace." The words are softly uttered, sincerely meant.

We sit in silence before the flickering and smoke-rich flame. When it burns down to fine gray ashes, our eyes readjust to darkness. Beyond us, unseen, cinder fields and lava flows stretch out toward the Little Colorado. Under a hazy glimmer of stars, we ride softly to sleep.

In the star-lit darkness before dawn, the slender cries of coyotes. As I drift back to sleep, my down jacket pillowing my head, I feel that the night is cool, not cold.

The sky is ashen and starless. Something, perhaps the Spirit invoked by last night's fire, prompts me to slip from the sleeping bag and step across the cinder floor.

As I look eastward through the empty eye of the doorway, the haze-thick horizon splits like a pomegranate. Barefoot on these savage ashes, I sense the dark roll of the earth down into day and my heart quickens. The sky glows like layered lava, and it seems as if the fire within the earth flows forth to meet the sun.

Alive in the dawning air and awake to its primal fire, I watch the great star rise. His is a crystalline beauty, six-sided and angular. Then the orange-red hexagon fattens to a central eye. I call to Lee. Together we watch the blood-red birth of day, the beginning of everything out of nothing. With awe we watch the sun's ascent, the land echoing his sky island song. I breathe the syllables lightly, as if in prayer.

While the star's divinity is dimmed by a mask of smoke, I dare to raise my high-powered binoculars. Dimples of solar storm swirl on the sun's orange disk. When I drop the binoculars, green circles of light swim along the burnt rocks. Stars of lime-green fire swim in my eyes where the god has entered.

When we can bear to watch no longer, we turn our backs on the stellar magnificence and climb the ramparts of the western wall. Like sentinels, we stand at the breast-high barrier and gaze across a land that the long light slowly takes—a cinder drifted landscape of parks and washes, ranges and ridges, juniper-dotted slopes, shrubby basins, and gray, hollow-cored craters. The light of his fire has created a world, and everything he touches is made holy.

WINTERING CROWS

I STRETCH AND LOOK OFF through a network of slender branches toward the white slopes and ridges of the Peaks. During my early morning vigil beside the Cherry Hill feeding station, I have observed, with half an eye, a high-level procession of crows, some flying overhead from south to north, others skimming the tips of the tallest pines from east to west.

Theirs is a presence marked by occasional caws and blackly graceful shapes slanting across the overcast sky. By twos and threes they perch, silent and watchful, in the thickly needled branches of the pines. I have yet to witness, however, the great black gathering of wings that characterize winter back in the farmlands of the Midwest.

Lee and I used to walk a path along the Huron River, not far from the double tracks of the New York Central, where spiked brown sumac had withered and dark green pines climbed the southern slope. Here, in the bleak days of late November, the wintering crows would come to roost and, in the cold gray dawn, whirl in masses above the rooftops of Ann Arbor.

To me they were the wild voice of the winter woods, and when I heard their daybreak calls, I could imagine their dark forms descending upon the roughly furrowed fields, swaggering through the pale stubble of corn stalks, or gleaning grain beside the haystacks, weathered and undercut by cattle. How suggestive their cries were of south forties, sagging fences, tumbledown sheds, and slate-gray skies! Shrewd and independent as individuals, in the tempered anarchy of their predawn flights, they displayed a bumptious, corn-fed sociability that was raucous with laughter and corvine confidence.

Their seasonal federation was fermentive to my mind, as the many became one and the long fight for survival seemed forgotten in the pure fellowship of flight.

I remember vividly a day when light was slow to come. As the sky grew grayer and the wind colder, their calls became louder. I lay for a moment thinking they are here again—from the four corners of the countryside, the crows have come, swartly pagan, hoarsely reveling.

Taking a robe and snugging the ties about

my waist, I stepped to the doorway. The sky was built for snowing, thickly overcast. I stood just outside, astounded by the uproar and ringing clatter of six hundred birds cawing together, at once and all between. The air pulsed with the beat of a thousand wings. I looked straight up into a drifting vortex of common crows whirl-pooling from west to east across the sky. As I watched, scores more rose from the rookery on the wooded hills above the Huron.

I cocked my head and listened, trying to distinguish each cough and caw, each tenor and baritone, alto and soprano in this massed Handelian chorus that hallelujahed to the first winter day. The ebony cloud rose and fell as it revolved like an unstable galaxy with spiraling arms. Theirs was the oblivious arrogance of old royalty, and they massed to assert their dominion over field and meadow, woodlot and barn, house and hillside.

With cold feet and numb face, I retreated toward the warmth of the threshold. Inside the doorway, I watched through the small hour of their revelry until, at last, the host dissolved. On separate, purposeful ways, out from the pine and shrub-oak hillside, they flew with steadily flapping wings. One mile south of where I stood and shivered, the wakened woods sighed forth a new and sleepy stillness. The wintering crows had gone, leaving token feathers under the pines. In all directions now, the world was wider, wilder, for their coming.

HAVASU CREEK

Havasu Creek

WE WALK LATE through Supai, past gardens of prickly Opuntia, past pale wands of horsetail. Underfoot lie red earth and the hoof-scattered droppings of horses; beside the trail, leafless cottonwoods and twiggy willows, sprawling vines and coarse-bladed grasses, mesquite and cushion moss awakened by winter rains.

After dark the stars of Orion flare above the canyon, then fade in the dawn. Red Zinger tea and hot oatmeal break our fast. Everywhere the sun shines, it is summer. Suited, we take the path down to the foot of Havasu Falls. Visitors sit or lie on ledges, bathed in the roar of the falls, absorbing the February sun.

Terraces of travertine contain the swirl of the creek and create blue-green pools filled with the sound of falling water. When I take to the long basin below the last dam, my body produces more heat than I need, and my skin prickles with fire. Under a full draft, I stroke down the narrow trough, reach the shallows, and return. I feel like a red giant radiating energy into the chill of outer space. Members of my family splash about me, swim and dive in a surge of foam, or rest, perched like dippers, on a chalky curve of calcium carbonate. Like a salmon heading upstream, I kick hard against the current, its constant pressure and flow. Glowing, exhilarated, alive, I sit on a ledge as lime-laced waters lather me in their froth and swirl.

Rested, half-dried, we eat pressed ham on whole-wheat, chocolate and cheese. Then we are off downstream, where Mooney explodes in continuous thunder. Mist and spray fill the basin with racing waves. Pearls of moisture cling to the carpeting moss. Wind-pummeled plants crouch beside curtains of frozen stone. Mud-slick limestone shines. One of my scouts leads the way from ledge to ledge, then down the vertical tunnel. Handholds and toeholds, spikes, chains, and bars. Our two youngest children, Roddy and Lael, wait on the terrace at the end of the first tunnel, their legs too short to reach the steps that follow.

Soon Lee and I discover a side canyon of fallen rocks, a slant-stone spring, and watercress. We hear the scale-descending song of a canyon wren and the call note of a dipper as it poises, wren-like, on a mid-stream stone. We climb to a dry falls blocked by a chock stone. Ahead, through a rock window, lies a pebbled basin and another rise of canyon wall.

The sound of water sinks into the seamless moment; time is the slow seepage of a spring in canyon shadow. We stand under the slanting boles of leafless, streamside trees with beauty before us, beauty behind us.

Now the first ford, with Beaver Falls two miles below. Addressing the truth of nature, we launch ourselves into the chill of Havasu Creek, stroke into the far shallows, then wade ashore, barefoot on the red earth, dripping, purely alone in a world of surpassing beauty.

A low cave at trailside. We rest with the stillness, the flow of the stream, its broad-leafed shrubs. A golden pendant falls across a bare shoulder, damp tendrils of hair touch the dry sand. Beauty above us, beauty below us. And then the simple ascent, up chains and rods into the haven of sun-sweet rock.

THE CACOMISTLE

WE ARE CAMPED ON AN ISLAND of sand in a sea of gray, water-rounded stones. A few yards north, the murky, melt-swollen waters of the creek race downhill toward the Verde. The roar of cascading water fills the canyon from the floodplain, with its sandstone inner walls, to the volcanic cliffs and lava-capped headland of Black Mountain.

Orion leans to the south. Towards morning I dream of a pack of pestering animals that violate our campsite and circle silently about the head of our sleeping bag. The moon's thin glow shows that they are not domestic dogs on a nocturnal lark, but western timber wolves whose eyes shine greenish-orange. When I rise up on one elbow and madly wave the six-volt lantern above my head, the wolves slink away, and the dream slowly fades.

Restarting yesterday's fire, I notice that the single slice of bread left in a plastic bag is missing. Gone also are the remaining oatmeal cookies we had saved to eat with the Pelican Punch tea.

Curious, I open the top of my backpack and find that the second loaf of Lee's home-baked cracked wheat is also missing. Scattered over the damp and level sand are small, round, five-toed, and clawless paw prints. Extending upstream from my pack are wavy lines—the sandy wake left by the slow passage of our loaf!

While water heats for breakfast, I turn a page of Lee's journal and sketch the tracks to scale. Hind and front paw prints are similar and show that the bandit lands with his feet close together in weasel-like bounds that average eighteen inches.

The robbery is the work of neither raccoon nor wood rat—this the tracks make plain. A name rings in my mind, but I will not know for certain till I'm back in my study, with Claus Murie's *Field Guide to Animal Tracks* open before me.

My son Russell and I follow the loaf-trail, losing it when it leaves the sand and crosses the flood-rolled boulders. The thief may have scaled a ten-foot cliff and scrambled up the gully to the south. If he did, he's one expert climber, I'll say that for the rascal. On this note, the search ends and the mystery remains.

The second night we bait him with sugar cookies, and I sleep with a lantern beside my head. Shrewdly, he comes early, between eleven and twelve, during our first sleep. When Robert, our elder son, gets up to check the stone, the cookies are already gone. Five times later that night, I wake from a light sleep and sweep the sand with the lantern's powerful beam. Nothing. He has eluded us.

His identity does not, however; now we know what to look for the next time we camp at Loch Nesta. The ringtail is rarely seen, so silent, stealthy, and nocturnal are his predatory habits. Farther south he prowls about under his Spanish/Indian name: cacomistle. Scientists know him as *Bassariscus astutus*, and astute he certainly is.

A relative of the raccoon and the coati, the ringtail is a slender, short-legged mammal with the pointed face of a fox and the prominent eyes and large, rounded ears of a lemur. He takes his English name from his long, bushy tail that is half of his thirty-inch length and is distinctly banded with black and white.

His coat is yellowish-gray; his eyes are rimmed with white, and his face and forehead streaked with black. His feet have semi-retractile claws and fur between their pads, and leave small five-toed tracks. When aroused, he may whimper or give a coughing bark similar to that of a fox. Since the adult ringtail weighs a modest two pounds, our bushy-tailed visitor stole a loaf of bread that was half his own weight!

The cacomistle is known to prefer the cliffs and ledges of steep-walled canyons in the upper Sonoran where oaks, cottonwoods, and sycamores deposit their leaves and broken branches in stream-swept piles that provide nesting sites for his rodent prey. Expert mousers, they also take insects, lizards, and birds, as well as cactus fruits and camper goodies. Sharing the raccoon's fondness for sugar, ringtails, though shy, were easily lured into camp by lonely prospectors who yearned for both companionship and effective vermin control.

Though winter floods have scoured the sacred datura from the sands of Loch Nesta, the cacomistle has come to us in the dark, silent and shrewd, fearless and friendly. Perhaps some night this spring, we shall meet him face to face.

NORTH TO THE HILLS

AS WE FOLLOW A FENCELESS route to the Peaks, we pass through open groves with their shadow thatch of pine needles; we cruise islands of pale gold grasses; and we watch the bronze and khaki of oak leaves as they whirl and skitter on the red-cindered road to TV Hill and Devil's Head.

North of the Elden Road, the rust of bracken stains the Celtic slopes of the roughly bouldered hills. Green, tufted tassels from the tips of the pines litter the wayside. The landscape is a tri-color composition. One part November's high clear blue; another the pagan green of black-boled and dog-haired pine; the third, the wheat, russet, and gray of the foreground grasses with their low-lying stones and scattered shrubs.

A tree squirrel sprints across the road while overhead a raven utters a hoarse, sunless croak as he quarters the chill wind. Then a pair of these sober birds circles above us, touching wingtips in the gliding turns of their aimless flight. Companionable and at ease, they seem to ride the gusts of the mountain wind for a purely personal pleasure. Roadside weeds harbor flocks of vesper sparrows who flash their white-trimmed tails in flight.

We turn north at the cairn and enter the shadowed canyon. Last week's snow lingers beside boulders and beneath the boles of fallen firs. The stretch of trail where we once camped is crusted with an inch of snow, and the hieroglyphs of animal tracks fill the canyon with a sense of life unwitnessed but clearly recorded. The small, neat prints of field mice. The light but regular leaps of a gray squirrel. The hurried, moonlit exclamations of a cottontail. Then, a traffic jam of turkey tracks.

I span one with my ungloved hand. Six inches from hind spur to tip of middle toe. It is the symmetrical print of a Thanksgiving gobbler. The flock of five to seven birds seems to have headed up canyon, then crossed the western ridge.

Last and largest of the tracks are the deep, double almonds of an adult mule deer. The evidence of the slate is clear—this canyon is a route to and from the high country, and we travel with a company whose wild presence is as palpable as the air.

Our pace slows on the ascent. My eyes have time to mark the fall of fir needles, the gray-green shades of lichen, the low, red leaves of creeping mahonia.

We reach the jeep trail at the head of the draw and look across the yellow waste of marsh grass to the wooded ridge on the far side. A pickup truck with a camper top moves slowly south along the primitive road. When it stops beside us, the driver asks the inevitable question: "Seen any deer?"

I have already prepared my answer. "No, nary a one."

Dry Lake Tank is clear—unmuddied by the recent fall of rain and snow. We will camp on the wooded ridge and enjoy the luxury of plentiful firewood and abundant water. We drop our packs where five large pines have layered the level soil. The wind sings overhead and sunlight angles in from the west.

Reaching under the clear plastic tarp, Lee gleans a harvest of pine stubs and decaying cones. The predicted low for this night is sixteen degrees, and we pitch our tent and rainfly with more than usual care. Unpressed by time or the approach of darkness, we relish the small tasks of setting up camp. Lee gathers dead branches while I saw lengths from a fallen pine. The folding handsaw has a short stroke, and I am glad to rest my arms after the fall of each log.

Other hunters cruise the hollow and return, disappointed, along Brookbank Road. I can hear their laboring engines a half mile away, and I wonder if this is how they hunt. Their four-wheel drive vehicles lurch slowly ahead with as much stealth as an American-made car can manage. Not one hunter gets out to muddy his feet or breathe the still, chill air of evening.

I set flat rocks against a weathered boulder whose surface scales away in concave slabs of lichened stone. As if determined not to be mistaken for quarry, our small fire broadcasts billows of pale gray smoke from a heap of snow-damp pine cones. Thus we announce our benign presence to the hunting world. As our water steams and boils, light climbs the guardian pines till only their tips glow in the sun.

Twenty minutes after the last hunters cruise by, we are startled by the sharp, close-hand report of a rifle. Someone has fired near or across the tank. The shot rings out at sundown, and I wonder if it serves to signal the deer that they have no more to fear from hunters for this day.

To the west, the last light flows down the rivers of the windfall night and the quiet stars appear. Like distant flares along the highway of our galaxy or like roadside reflectors that return the faint rays of our sun, the stars, on this moonless night, pierce the chill sky from unimaginable distances.

But our tent is close and warm, and the

thick-boled pines hold us in their friendly circle through the long and restful night.

In the infant light of morning, the "chink-chink" of a tree squirrel high over our heads. Warm within our tent, Lee and I are in no hurry to face the cold. If we let the earth spin awhile, it will sink below the sun.

The sun, I think—for thoughts flow freely in a mind close to sleep—is our paternal star, the great allgod of earth, the primal source, seed-bringer and cloud-mover, and patron of all the saints. He flares over TV Hill and Turkey Park, sings down through the pines with a pale eastern voice, and breaks the chill of this long November night. On a cold morning, we all worship the sun.

I assume a Promethean role and set about the chill task of building, like Jack London's hero, a small fire. Though no sun in magnitude, it will be closer and more serviceable.

I scrape out the ashes, then crumple a bed of paper towels. Next I gather pine cones that are brittle with cold and heap them upon the paper. Though I breathe upon the timid flame, the frozen cones refuse to kindle and the fire fails. Having used the last of the Scott towels, I look about for other tinder.

I can see only that, high in the western sky,

the waning moon is up for breakfast. Though he does not come down for stewed peaches or Morning Thunder tea, he seems to smile when I build a lean-to of kitchen matches and roof it with small dry twigs that flame up and thaw the cones till, resin-rich, they burn with a bright and windy roar.

My legs receive the warmth as my gloved hands set the aluminum grill in place. Water that has slept with us in the tent splashes freely into the bail-handled pot. Pine smoke swells in a sudden draft and blinds my eyes. I blink and turn away to the cold, smokeless air. Unsweetened, the peaches bubble in their thick and natural syrup.

Lee sits on the old, dust-gray nylon tarp that serves as ground cloth to tie her laces. The smell of food and the crackle of the fire have brought her forth. She wonders if the hunters—this being a holiday—will be out in force. In the hour since dawn, not a single vehicle has climbed Brookbank Road, and this Monday seems an Armistice Day for the deer.

While waiting for the water to boil, I take the binoculars and scan the southern horizon. Above and beyond the draw, I can see Mt. Elden and the sticks of pines left from the Radio Fire of two summers ago. I make a mental note to scoop up canteen cups full of snow from the north side of a boulder and mound over the remains of our fire till it steams as thoughtfully as an old gentleman puffing on his meerschaum.

The closed circle of the binoculars suggests a telescopic sight, and I imagine for a moment that I have come to hunt these ridges and hollows. I descend the slope to the meadow with a slow and watchful walk, weapon ready to aim and fire. At the ridge crest I stand like Natty Bumpo in half shade and scan the glade beyond. The open woods are patched by snow and sand-yellow clumps of withered grass. The hollows retain more moisture than the slopes, and here the soil is black and bog-soft. The morning is still and windless; the sun a constant, reassuring presence.

I see, on thin sweeps of crusty snow, the step marks of mule deer—clear trails of cleft hoofs that follow the slope like a line of logical thought. On the rocky south slope of the ridge, I find, beside a fallen pine, clustered lumps of deer scat. Strolling back to breakfast, I invent for myself long, agile ears that turn like weather vanes to catch the faintest whisper in the wind. My nostrils flare at each strange scent, and I comfort myself with the thought that a rifle bullet would not travel far in these woods. I stop to browse on an oak twig; the brittle leaves leave a smoky taste in my mouths.

I move slowly ahead; the melt-soft soil yields underfoot but is firmer in tree shadow, hard where the sun never reaches. I cross a tire trail, snow track of a hunter's helper machine, and, curious, I follow it for thirty yards. The trail peters out at the head of the draw. Emergent rocks rise angular and weathered; the ravine is crossed by fallen timbers. It darkly descends the north slope, sheltered and shadowed. A sanctuary for such as I. Glad to be alive, I lift my head and snuff the clear, cold air.

WALNUT CANYON

IF YOU WOULD KNOW the spirit of Walnut Canyon, haunted as ruins are by human hopes and faces, stand in the cool of the midday overhang, some terrace where the children played. Savor the shade of a Douglas Fir or sit in the shadow of a Gambel oak and gaze cross canyon till the lamp-black smudge against the limestone ledge becomes a house of maize and beans, squash and sunflowers. Then lift up your eyes to the angular, towered rocks above you—mineral-stained and flecked with the red of penstemon and paintbrush, mottled with the greens of rock mat and serviceberry, cliff-rose and yucca.

Look downward, inward, to the cross-bedded sandstone and see it suddenly soften to a living dune slowly shifting its bulk along the shore. Swim in this unremembered sea for a million years, never tiring, while death lays down these ledges one life at a time; and the pure persistence of water brings all things to this premature dusk of locust and walnut, willow and box elder. Listen, while a great horned owl, tufted ears upright, anticipates a further darkness.

Save for a rare spring when Lower Lake Mary floods and Walnut Creek flows again to the spirit songs of the Sinagua, mule deer trace the creek bed, browse in the violet-green light of swallows that slash the upper air as they hawk the invisible.

Now take the rim trail, since the swift flyers find the air here unfenced and insect-laden in the updraft. Walk through the low and pleasant forest of pinyon and juniper and, in your mind, collect, since you will need them, plants and roots that are firewood, food, and fiber, medicines, dyes, and drugs. Be pleased by the blue-black of the elderberries, the rich yellow of the sulfur flower, and the frank utility of yucca, mountain mahogany, and Apache plume. Delight in the white and yellow fragrance of flowering cliff-rose, and in the fruit of currant and wild grape.

Enjoy the Steller's jay's spiraling approach through the branches of the one-seed juniper, then his spread-winged swoop and pounce as he captures your crust, and, with a pirate's swagger, wings away.

Finally, stand in the cloud-colored light of an overlook, hands on the metal railing, and contemplate the wooded ridge of Anderson

Mesa, thickly green and elf-ridden. Watch, in the high, sun-struck air, the slow revolutions of turkey vultures. As they drift closer, they show you what they are—six-foot soarers and tireless scavengers with heads nakedly red and eyes coldly clinical.

Admire the spread of their primaries as, feathers splayed and rippled, they slant by, indifferent to your presence and infinitely professional. Each bird passes in a black silence of grace, then settles in his wilderness roost. Seeing them again, living this canyon again, your spirit sings, stirs the small stones of the broken ledges.

CANYON WALLS,
FLOODPLAIN TREES

IN LOVE WITH THIS LAND, I sit and look upstream—one of the two directions sight can flow along a high-banked and wooded creek. Beyond the green tendrils of a canyon grape that trails down from its host tree to touch the water, is the north bank's rust red wall. Like hair on the head of a balding man is its thin fringe of velvet mesquite and catclaw acacia.

My eyes drift upward to the far walls of the greater canyon. Lizard Peak, an erosional promontory, raises its angular head against the azure, infinite sky. My binoculars sweep the canyon rim, which is guarded by motionless sentinels—stalked agave and stick-figure ocotillo.

Above the cliff's volcanic ramparts, the sun patrols in his endless round. His torch lightens the dark layers of lava, shines on gullies, rockslides, and unstable aprons of dark gray stones. Everywhere is seen the unfinished work of gravity.

Add to this picture varied shades of green—
the thicket woods of chaparral, troops of
prickly pear, pale leaves of shrub oak, dark
clumps of juniper. With a full sweep of your
brush, shape a sky so uniformly blue that it
delights the imagination; a sky the shade of
Homer's wine-dark sea.

After you have done the sky, the sheer rock
walls, the long slopes of desert shrub, the
shadowed side canyons and ravines, the next
touch from your palette must be for the crusts
of sandstone breaking through in ledges and
isolated cliffs. These should be Oak Creek and
Sedona red. In the near foreground, to add
depth to the picture, draw, with deft strokes of
a finely tapered brush, the dark gray, deeply
ridged trunks of young trees—cottonwood,
willow, ash, sycamore, and walnut. Color the
woods' high canopy a thin and plaintive green.

Here, many of the higher branches are
leafless or stricken, as if drained of vitality by
the loss of supporting roots. Older trees raise
their leaf-scant branches above a river-stone
wall whose unnatural regularity suggests a
railroad embankment. A flood-downed ash
sends up a rank of living branches that bear
the single-winged seeds called keys. Beside it,
other veterans of the flood put forth leaves in
another season of sun. As I watch, a muffled
crack breaks the windless silence of the
riparian wood, and a curved piece of outer bark

falls from the newly bared branch of a sycamore.

Now the sunlight fades on the fire-burnt crest, its columnar blocks complexly fractured, weathered, and split. Downstream, dusk invites the little brown bats that cluster at the westward bend of the creek. From the twilight gloom of an old cottonwood, they dart out in flight so quick and trembling my lightweight binoculars cannot track them.

As the sun sets, its last light leaving the orange-red sandstone walls, a great gold moon rises in the east. When it tops the thin-leafed branches, Lee and I drift off in easy slumber. Sprawled on the top of our open sleeping bag, we dream a midsummer dream in the moon's full light.

WILDERNESS WINGS

BACKLIGHTED BIRDS, so many I cannot count them. Unidentifiable floating objects, black against the white gold of the lake.

Through my binoculars, I look southwest across the sun-glimmered surface of Lower Lake Mary. Thousands of migrant waterfowl, in a wash of linear motion, ride the rippled waters. Like vessels from random, unmoored fleets, they pursue their own way, or, in long strings, churn south through rafts of bay ducks. I watch a diving duck take a taxi run, his webbed feet pattering the water and leaving a wake of wave-sparkle.

Always in my ears the mutterings of waterfowl, the clutter and cluck of restless birds. I close my eyes to listen to the wheezes, whistles, and squeaks of the drakes and the subdued, deep-throated quacks of the females. From close in come the call notes and feeding sounds of marsh ducks as they dabble among pond weeds or tip forward, tails up, to probe the shallows.

All this is seen and heard in a few, fast-flying minutes while the sun, a blend of Gandalf gray and winter orange, wades through a shoal of clouds and sinks below the ragged edge of the pines. As the surface light dims, stranger, wilder sounds come from on high. I look eastward where the lake thins to winter meadow, then lift the binoculars to scan the sky. Turning, I call back toward the car, "Canada geese!"

Lee joins me as a score of geese in a lopsided 'V' come winging up from the southeast. The full, steady strokes of their wings count a cadence that impresses with its sense of purpose. They bank in a half circle to scout a dozen dark, long-necked shapes that call to them from the far shallows. Still on their first great turn, they pass to the north, as if heading for Marshall Lake. But in another moment they are overhead, their gray-brown bodies borne by deeply bowed wings, their black necks stretching forward. Passing to the south a second time, they turn steeply, just clearing the tips of the pines. Suddenly their wings cease beating and they begin a swift slant downward on the last leg of this day's journey.

Braking against the air, they fan their wings in a feathered flurry, then drop breastward into the water. The splash of their collective landing, though muted by two hundred yards, blossoms into waves of sound that boom outward across the lake till dimmed by a clamor of goose greetings—spontaneous assertions of solidarity, identity, and purpose. At last the tumult subsides into social babblings.

How far have they flown today, I wonder, and where will they rest tomorrow? Will they follow the slow steps of spring till they reach Fort Resolution and the shores of the Great Slave Lake?

My pleasure in this wilderness spectacle is undiminished as flight after flight of Canada geese appears to the south and, following the same pattern of approach and descent, comes to rest upon the evening waters. Though light is beginning to wane, the large twilight factor of my binoculars allows me to witness some fascinating details of goose behavior.

Now thirty geese in a broken line sweep over the resting grounds and turn south to complete the second of their great circles. Suddenly the 'caboose goose', as if tired of trailing his fellows, rebelliously wheels about, asserting an unsuspected talent for leadership, and heads for the Hampton Roads of his heart. The consternation of his fellow honkers is amusing as, with a confused beating of wings, the line reverses itself in flight and follows its new, self-appointed leader on the long slant down to the anchorage.

Another flock arrives on the scene, this one full of frustrated leaders. Wings almost touching, a black knot of birds crowd together at the apex of the 'V', each vying for the point position. Their frantic struggle for precedence suggests the finish of a hundred meter dash for Leda's Olympic Gold. Indifferent to fame or above such folly, a straggle of geese lazes behind the leaders.

As each flight lands, there is the usual exchange of greetings, and then the Canadians settle down for sleep. However, as soon as they hear the contact calls of an incoming flight, the resting geese wake with a rush of social excitement. Their pitched cries of "We're here! We're here! Come down! Come down!" rise to a crescendo as their fellows swing low overhead and then drop heavily into the shallows.

At last, gregarious in the gathering darkness, three separate bands converge. A half hundred at least, they fall into an orderly line, none pushing for precedence or bolting from place, each obedient to the larger will of the group. My heart stirs to the miracle of the flock as each goose, at the same instant, stills the powerful stroke of his pinions and, wings gracefully curved, glides down to his companions, settles upon the mothering waters.

THE HILLS OF HOME

THESE MOUNTAINS, never out of sight, are never out of mind. Their presence—brooding, reclusive, and strangely inviting—hammers the soul. Moving away from each other, they create, like retreating stars, a cosmic emptiness. As sound determines silence, their swelling flanks and rounded ridges set limits to sight, spawn a sense of space acutely pleasurable. Set in a blue grama rangeland where the small green of yucca mimics a forest, these ancient hills possess a religious significance. Each comes with its own emotional halo; each is a psychic presence. A few ranch houses, dark and sightless and lonely, sit far back from the ribbon of Arizona 82. Their remoteness from the road suggests a preference for solitude and space.

Some of the hills ease upward out of the earth; others leap to their feet with a terrible energy. One small-scale mountain lies close to the highway—seems open, inviting, accessible. Stop here, it says, and climb. But beneath its superficial charm lies an ancient eccentricity of form. With the others, it shares a mystique that at night, under a full moon, might be unbearable. Changing Lady, Changing Man, these shapes suggest transcendent things. The mind spins inward and meets the heart halfway. Form without function, leftover land, a knot in the wood of the world, a core of stony truth.

I want to stop the car and kneel at the edge of the earth. Dim wraiths, long vanished forms, rise from the shadowed draws. Who are those that stand sentinel on the rough thumbs and rounded knobs of weathered rock, their tilted strata rising from the prairie sea like the prows of sinking ships? Perhaps they are Apache braves bent on vengeance for the betrayal of Cochise, for the shame-stained flag of truce.

What more can I say of these mountains that, as Richard Sheldon writes, try every possible position and finally sleep with their backs to one another? Rune stones, erosion mounds, many-shaped, mysterious in every light except that of noon, lofty earth music in changeless motion.

Far to the south lie the foothills of the Huachucas, the slow rise to the borderland. Surely those distant tracings are not roads but ridgebacks branded by fire-trails visible from twenty miles away. I look up to where the pines begin, to where the Gambel oaks are shedding their November leaves.

Forty-five years have gone, like the ghosts and graves of Fort Crittenden, where we stopped to read the roadside marker. There, south of Sonoita, we found only the silence of a late autumnal grassland and memories of sycamores and cottonwoods limp with the stillness of July. The hoarse buzz of flies; Patagonia and the pungent report of firecrackers; the arc of sparklers through the night sky.

My head rests on the leather upholstery of our Franklin touring car. Hills mask the stars. The hills of home.

About the Author

Judson D. McGehee is an emeritus professor of English. Born in Akron, Ohio, he lived the nomadic life of an army child and experienced a diversity of environments, from the humid Panama Canal Zone at Fort Davis to the arid Arizona desert of Fort Huachuca.

After a tour of duty in the U.S. Army, he received a B.A. in Creative Writing and an M.A. in American Literature at Stanford University. A two-year fellowship took him to the University of Michigan, where he completed his Ph.D. in English.

During a thirty-year career at Northern Arizona University, he taught English and Creative Writing and served as advisor for the university's literary magazine *Pine Knots*. From 1976 to 1987, he wrote a weekly column "Northland Nature" for the *Arizona Daily Sun*.

He resides in Flagstaff, Arizona with his wife Lyn and their dog Timber. For the latest on his publications, visit www.judsonmcgehee.com.